Calling All Souls—

You Do Matter!

COLLECTIVE WISDOMS

Fiona Frances

ISBN: 978-1-4269-9326-8 (sc)
ISBN: 978-1-4269-9327-5 (e)

Trafford rev. 01/18/2012

 www.trafford.com

North America & international
toll-free: 1 888 232 4444 (USA & Canada)
phone: 250 383 6864 ♦ fax: 812 355 4082

Dedication

My Husband and Daughters

Oprah Winfrey

Tyler Perry

Jaycee Dugard

… for teaching us about courage, strength and hope!

CALLING ALL SOULS—YOU DO MATTER!

Calling all Souls—You Do Matter! is a unique collection of wisdom, common sense and golden rules intended to lighten and inspire your soul's journey here on Earth. It will guide you in the co-creation of your best self by teaching you to trust in your intuition, to create a Life Plan, and to act on inspired guidance. You will learn that what you focus on and what you commit to is what will bring the results you seek. Positive thoughts create positive actions. And by simply making the choices that are right for you, you co-create your happiness and success in life. You define you! You and only you define your life's mission and purpose. There is a great goodness about what you can bring into the world to make it a better place.

You do matter, you do count and you are loved very much by your Creator. You are very important here on this earth -and at this time. Your spirit-soul has been placed here for a reason; to learn something, to share something, to teach something. You have been blessed with special gifts and talents that only you can open and share with the world. Your gift back is what you have created with your skills and talents. The happiest people in the world are those who follow their passion.

Your Creator is your FAITH source. Your Creator is who and what guides your conscious decisions in making choices. Your Creator is who you believe to be the source of the Divine Love Energy in your heart and soul. And, if you are not sure at this time who your Creator is and what that means, then substitute the God you worship, your parents, grandparents, teacher or guardian.

If one advances confidently in the direction of his own dreams, and endeavors to live the life which he has imagined, he will meet with a success unexpected in common hours.

Henry David Thoreau

Creator/Divine Being/Deity/God: most often conceived of as the supernatural creator and overseer of the universe with infinite knowledge, unlimited power, present everywhere, and eternal, **an energy that can neither be created nor destroyed.**

Human Being: Human is form. Being is formless. Humans are a trinity of body, mind and spirit. Humans are the only beings with a free-will. Humans have a highly developed brain, capable of idea, reason and logic. Humans have the ability to act with appropriate judgment. The human Body is made up of organs, which are made up of cells, which are made up of molecules, which are made up of atoms, which are made up of energy **-an energy that can neither be created nor destroyed.**

Energy: Each and every thing is made of energy. Energy is power which may be translated into motion, overcoming physical change. The energy of the universe is constant and cannot be created or destroyed. Life on Earth is driven by energy. All living things are made up of carbon molecules, which are made up **of energy and that matter is neither created nor destroyed.**

Karma: The universal principal of cause and effect, action and reaction for example: if one extends goodness, one will receive goodness; if one extends negativity, one will receive negativity. Karma is **not** fate, for humans act with free-will creating their own destiny. Karma is **not** punishment but a consequence of natural acts.

Law of Attraction: The most powerful law in the universe, and key component in the greatest teachings in the world for several millennia. Law of Attraction states: What you choose to think about and what you are feeling is what you are attracting into your life and what is moving you toward your destiny. Consciously paying attention to your thoughts, feelings and choices is key to co-creating your best self and best life.

CREATOR

Your Creator is your FAITH source. Your Creator is what guides your conscious decisions in choosing right or wrong. Your Creator is what you believe to be the source of the Divine Love Energy in your heart and soul. If you are not sure what that means, then substitute your God, parents, grandparents or guardian.

FAITH

Faith is the inspiration that guides you. Faith is TRUST that there is something larger than you in the universe, a Divine Love and a Divine Creator. **Faith is believing that your Creator dwells within you as you.** Faith is believing in your inner-voice and having the confidence to act upon what you hear. Faith is knowing that your Divine presence here on Earth will make a positive difference.

YOU

You are LOVE. You are a loving human being. You are the integration of body, mind and spirit-soul. You have a conscious mind, a free-will to make choices. You control your thoughts, words and actions. You shape your destiny. You are the magnificence that creates the best you and the best life for you. You are love, faith and hope. You are life!

.

YOU DO MATTER!

Did you know? You matter!

You do! You matter very much!

You matter more than you can believe!

You matter today, tomorrow and forever!

Even if you don't think you matter, you matter.

You matter in this life, in this world and at this time.

You matter whether you are pretty or plain, rich or poor!

Your Creator loves you for who you are not for anything you have!

You matter regardless of your religion, race, culture, or sexual orientation!

You matter just the way you are because that is how your Creator made you!

Your Creator, your God, dwells within you as you!

There is something unrepeatable and mysterious about being you.

You matter because you are unique and uniqueness matters!

Let no one make you feel unworthy. You are worthy!

What others think of you is none of your business!

There is no other person in the world like you!

You are worthy of all life's treasures!

You never have to prove it.

You are worthy.

Believe!

WHO ARE YOU?

You are love.

You are a loving human being.

And, we are all connected by that love.

The very heart within you is about love and faith.

Your Creator wants you to know that you are loved!

It is very important to love yourself, as the Creator loves you!

You are lovable, loving and worthy of all things!

Great things can happen in your life!

You are love, faith, and hope.

All you have to do is…

Believe!

WHAT ARE YOU?

You are...

Body, mind and spirit-soul.

Human is form. Being is formless.

The body is the physical instrument.

The mind is your thinking, your thoughts.

You are the integration of body, mind and spirit-soul.

You have a conscious mind, a free-will to make choices.

The spirit-soul is your consciousness, your awareness.

You are love, faith and hope. You are life!

You are a loving human being.

You are love.

YOU ARE BODY.

The body is your temple.

The body is the physical instrument.

It is important to take care of your body.

It is important to love and accept your body.

Your Creator has blessed you with your body, your temple.

Your Creator is pleased when you treat your body with respect.

Your body requires rest, exercise, nutritious foods and positive thoughts.

Your body is the visible instrument that houses your mind and spirit-soul.

Your body is a perfect mirror of the Divine Creator, who resides within you as you.

Your body contains all the energy you will need to accomplish your goals.

It is important to see beauty in all parts of your body.

Choose to think healthy and positive thoughts.

Your health is a product of your thoughts.

You are in control of your body.

Take care of your body.

Love your body.

Love yourself.

Love.

SUPER FOOD FOR SUPER HEALTH

- Blueberries
- Cantaloupe
- Strawberries
- Oranges
- Peppers
- Broccoli
- Salmon
- Oats
- Quinoa
- Kale
- Sweet Potato
- Almonds
- Beans
- Pumpkin
- Soy
- Spinach
- Green Tea
- Tomatoes
- Walnuts
- Yogurt

BODY FACTS

Your body, your health is a product of your thoughts and emotions.

Your body recoils from what is bad and leans toward what is good.

Your thoughts influence your emotions and your biochemistry.

Your body requires adequate rest, exercise, nutritious foods.

You have the enormous potential to re-wire your brain.

Choose to think positive and healthy thoughts.

Positive thoughts equal a healthy body.

Take care of yourself!

Eat nutritious foods.

Think positive.

Exercise.

Learn.

Play.

Rest.

Special Note: You must treat your body with respect. Never let anyone be disrespectful to your body. If anyone is disrespectful or abusive to your body, or your person, you must tell a parent, a teacher or if you want to remain anonymous phone a help line. No parent, guardian or friend should ever touch your private parts in an improper way. If something does not feel right to you then you must talk to someone who can help you! You must protect yourself from the harm of others. Remember to share all your worries with your Creator and ask for guidance. And, you also must never be disrespectful to anyone. Never bully anyone. Never bear false witness against someone. Never commit an act of violence, physically or emotionally to another, for example, murder, rape or incest. Remember the universal principle of Karma: cause and effect, action and reaction - if one extends negativity, one will receive negativity.

All that we are is a result of what we have thought.

Buddha

YOU ARE MIND.

The mind is your reason and logic.

The mind is your thinking, your thoughts.

Seven is the age of reason and understanding.

Seven is the age to understand intention and purpose.

You have a free-will to choose your thoughts and feelings.

You choose to think, talk, and act positively. Choose positive.

~What you think, say and do must all be the same~

Choose to say what you mean and mean what you say.

You control your feelings, thoughts and actions.

Only you choose *how* you want to think.

Your thoughts create your experiences.

Choose to think and act positive.

You become what you believe.

You are what you think!

You shape your destiny.

~Think~

Positive.

Productive.

Abundant.

Thought

There is nothing more than thought.

Deed follows word and word follows thought.

Always aim at harmony of thought and word and deed.

Always aim at purifying your thoughts and everything will be well.

Mahatma Gandhi

YOU ARE SPIRIT-SOUL.

The spirit-soul is your inner-being.

The spirit-soul is your consciousness, your awareness.

Your thoughts are your consciousness, your awareness.

Consciousness is the part of your mind that chooses your thoughts.

No one else in the entire universe has your spirit-soul, your inner-being.

The spirit-soul, your inner-being, exists beyond this time and into eternity.

The world we create for ourselves is the result of our thoughts.

When you choose your thoughts, you choose your actions.

This is how you co-create the life you desire.

You are responsible for your choices.

Commit to making your life work.

You become what you believe.

Believe in your spirit-soul.

Believe you matter!

Believe!

SELF ESTEEM

I am a good person.

I love and trust myself.

I am proud of who I am.

I celebrate my uniqueness.

I accept myself for who I am.

I am the best I can be in each moment.

I can discipline myself to reach my goals.

I treat myself the way I want to be treated.

I accept the fact that I do not have to fit in.

I accept my imperfections as opportunities to learn.

I take responsibility for my own well-being.

SPIRITUALITY

I am one with my Divine Creator.

I trust the Divine guidance I am receiving.

I co-create my reality with my Divine Creator.

I trust in my highest self and listen to what I hear.

My presence on earth makes a positive difference.

I am ready and willing to be the best person I can be.

When I trust my Divine Creator within, anything is possible.

I accept my imperfections as opportunities to learn.

I am able to accomplish anything I choose.

I am committed to making my life work.

I take responsibility for my choices.

I am committed to my Life Plan.

I am in charge of my own life.

I trust the decisions I make.

I know who I am.

I accept myself.

I love myself.

Love.

If you think you are too small to have an impact,

try going to bed with a mosquito.

Anita Roddick

WHY ARE YOU HERE?

You are here to give and receive love.

You are here to be the co-creator in your life.

You are here to share all your skills and talents with the world.

There is a great goodness about what you can bring into the world!

Your spirit-soul is here on Earth to grow and develop -to learn life lessons.

You are here to live a conscious life; to live life on purpose and meaning.

It is up to you to think, say and do the things that will make you happy.

It is up to you to allow good things to come to you.

You stand in your own light, so make it shine!

The point of your life is to understand that!

All you have to do is…

Think Positive.

Talk Positive.

Act Positive.

Just try it!

You create your own universe as you go along.

Winston Churchill

CO-CREATION

You are what you think.

You become what you believe.

What you focus on creates your feelings.

Your feelings create your thoughts and actions.

What you think, is what you say, and what you do.

When you choose your thoughts, you choose your actions.

The world you create for yourself is a result of your thoughts!

This is how you co-create your reality, your life.

Take the first step in faith; you don't need to see the whole staircase; just take the first step.

Dr. Martin Luther King

LIFE PLAN

Define your life.

Write your script.

It takes a little work.

What are your thoughts?

What is your gut telling you?

Release your worries to your Creator.

Only you can decide what it is you want.

Your inner-world creates your outer-world.

Envision the life you want to have for yourself.

Use your free-will to make choices for you.

Dream on until your dreams come true.

You can do it. Have faith!

Make a Life Plan.

Dream!

How to Create a Life Plan.

You are the masterpiece of your own life. You are the magnificence that creates the best you and best life for you. Your spirit-soul resonates with a deep sense of passion and conviction and it tells you what it is you want and desire. You and only you can decide upon your life's mission and purpose; it is up to you to discover your work and then to dedicate yourself to it. Begin now.

1. **Ask** yourself questions daily and let the answers come to you, for example:
    a)   What are my wants, needs and desires?
    b)   What do I want my life's mission and purpose to be?
    c)   How do I want to use my skills and talents?

2. **Envision** the life you want to lead. Get still. Go to your feeling place. Focus on what it is you want to bring into your life. Let your mind shape the very thing you perceive. Generate the feeling of having it now. *Dream.*

3. **Want it.** What is your heart's desire? What do you want? Trust your gut feelings and thoughts. Create a vision board by drawing or cutting out pictures of the things you want to bring into your life.

Imagination is everything. It is the preview of life's coming attractions.

Albert Einstein

4. **Declare it.** Make a Life Plan. First write down what it is you are grateful for and then write down what it is you intend to have in your life. What do you want your life's mission and purpose to be? *(Life Plan journal on back page.)*

5. **Take Action.** Act on your intuition. Follow your inner guidance and act on an inspired idea. Take the first step and then the next. Continuously, research, learn and practice what you are passionate about. Just take that first step toward your light *–and see what happens. Remember to practice, practice and practice.*

6. **Release and Trust.** Trust that the right situations will present themselves to you. Remain calm and have patience.

Your Creator has blessed you with special gifts that only you can open. Your gift back is what you have created with those gifts. You are placed where you are for a reason, to learn something, to share something, to teach something. It is never too late to start. Yesterday is done. Only NOW exists. Start NOW.

If you compare yourself with others…

there will always be greater and lesser persons than yourself.

Max Ehrman

BE THE BEST YOU!

Never worry about what others may think.

Do what is right for you. Express yourself.

Just be the best YOU that you can be!

Confidence makes a beautiful person!

Strive to be your best self.

Be Adventurous.

Be Courageous.

Be Optimistic.

Be Ingenious.

Be Creative.

Be Yourself.

Be Original.

Be Genuine.

Be Fearless.

Be Funny.

Be Happy.

Be Proud.

Believe.

Be!

There is no security in life. There is only opportunity.

Douglas McArthur

ABUNDANCE

You make you abundant.

It's okay to make lots of money.

You have the skills and talents required.

You are worthy just the way you are, rich or poor.

You are responsible for creating your financial success.

No matter how much money you have, your Creator loves you.

Commit to continuously learning and improving your skills.

Making money also lets you help many others who are in need.

You are accountable for managing your money honestly and responsibly.

Your worth as a person is not connected to how much money you have.

You can be proud of your hard work and enjoy an abundant life.

The happiest people are those who do what they love each day.

It is okay to start at the bottom and work your way up.

Money is great, but it doesn't guarantee happiness.

Never take what does not belong to you.

There is enough for everyone.

Set your money goals.

Just start!

GO!

"Genius is one per cent inspiration and ninety-nine per cent perspiration. Accordingly, a 'genius' is often merely a talented person who has done all of his or her homework."

&

Inspiration can be found in a pile of junk. Sometimes, you can put it together with a good imagination and invent something.

&

The three things that are most essential to achievement are common sense, hard work and stick-to-it-iv-ness.....

&

Many of life's failures are experienced by people who did not realize how close they were to success when they gave up.

Thomas Edison

Life can be very complicated.

You need to know *now* what it is you want out of life, in order for you to get what it is you want. Soon enough the world will tempt you with poor choices and negative messages. You will be influenced by the internet, television, movies and music. It will also come from unlikely sources, such as, family members, friends, strangers and even neighbors. You need to believe in yourself right *now*. You need to be ready to handle life's tricky situations for example things like, peer-pressure or street gangs. You and only you can decide what is right for you. Use your free-will to define you! Create your Life Plan now. Choose to live your life *on* purpose and *with* meaning, be aware of each choice you make in your life along with its outcome and consequence. Every action has a reaction. **Never surrender your free-will** *(your thinking, logic and judgment)* over to someone or something. Your free-will is your gift.

You may never know what results come from your action, but if you do nothing, there will be no results.

Gandhi

LIFE CIRCUMSTANCES

We are all born into our life's circumstances, for example: our parents, culture, religion and the community where we live. You may or you may not like your present circumstances, regardless, it is still your responsibility to make honorable choices for yourself. Trust that you are exactly where you are meant to be. Believe that you can co-create your best life. You define you. Challenge yourself to see what it is you can create with your life. Start now. **Your Creator helps those who help themselves.**

1. Release your worries to your Creator.
2. Tell yourself that you are a survivor.
3. Ask yourself, "What actions do I need to take to make the necessary changes in my life?"
4. Set a goal to study and work hard. Learn something new each day.
5. Save your money.
6. Be patient.

Only you know what it is that *you* want out of life, but if your thinking is, "*it will never happen for me,*" then it *never will* because you will have made a no-plan to journey to a new life. Start over now, rethink, redo, and reinvent yourself continuously.

Your inner-world creates your outer-world -what you focus on and what you commit to is what will give you the results you are seeking. Commit to constantly learning and growing. Commit to using your skills and talents. Commit to being abundant. Commit to helping others. Trust in the fact that you have the ability to do this. You have the ability to do this. You are the "someone" who should be doing the "something." Have faith in yourself. Make a Life Plan. Study hard. Work hard. Have patience, it takes time! Believe that your life will get better and it will get better!

LIFE SITUATIONS

Never surrender your free-will to alcohol, drugs, gangs, cults, smoking, teenage pregnancy, abusive relationships or sexual favors, because they all keep you in poor spirit and poverty. Poor choices rob you of the ability to become the best you. Have courage and be ready to tell your friends, "just not my thing." Get busy with your Life Plan.

Illegal Drug Use takes away your ability to be in control of your life. You can become addicted to drugs and get involved in crimes like stealing to pay for them. You could be sent to jail and have no freedom or choices. There is no happy drink or happy pill. True happiness only comes from within. Crack the books and not cocaine.

Illegal drug use:

- Impairs your free-will.
- Harms your body and brain.
- Takes away your personal freedom.
- Wastes your money and your chance for having a better life.

Teenage Pregnancy – Protect yourself and be responsible for your actions. There are no easy options once pregnant or HIV positive. Plan a family for your future, after your education, and when you have a job. The better educated the father and the mother the better educated the baby. You and your children are worthy of a life other than cyclical poverty. Save yourself for someone you love as an adult. You BOTH deserve to grow up first. Enjoy being a teenager.

Gangs – Joining a gang means surrendering to gang-think or gang consciousness. You will now have to think and act like someone else wants you to – even if it means breaking the law or breaking moral codes of conduct. Negative actions bring dishonor upon you. Develop the strength and the courage to be true to yourself, your Creator and your community.

Bullying –You never have the right to bully someone or make someone else feel that they do not matter. Bullying is self-hatred projected onto another person. You **never** have the right to intentionally hurt someone with words or actions; *it is dishonorable*. Remember the universal principle of Karma; if one extends negativity, one will receive negativity.

QUESTIONS?

1. **Do we always feel loved?** No, you may not always feel loved, but know that you are always loved by your Creator. You are very important and you do matter on this earth and at this time. And on the days that you are sad or down –*and we all have these days,* take a time-out to release your worries to your Creator. Know that it is okay to feel your feelings. Have a positive chat with yourself, and then get back to the business of your life. Tell yourself that things will get better and focus on the good in your life. Get busy with your Life Plan. Problem solve with questions like, "What steps can I take now to change my situation?" Remember that no matter how long or how hard the journey, stay focused on your goals to have the life you desire. It is up to each individual to make the necessary changes in their life. First, start by being grateful for what is presently good in your life so you can bring more of that into your life. Hang in there to see what it is you can create with your life. Dedicate yourself to reaching your goals.

2. **Is life easy?** Life is a challenge. Life's hardships develop our inner-strength and character. Our hardships develop the courage we need to bring about the necessary changes needed in our life and then to eventually bring it to others. It is your responsibility to make plans and goals for your life. No matter what your life situation, you are responsible for doing your soul's work here on earth. Use your life experiences to improve yourself. Listen to your inner-voice for guidance.

3. **What if I do not feel happy?** When you are not happy about a situation, talk to someone who will listen and understand, for example; a parent, teacher or friend. Release your worries to your Creator. Listen to your inner-voice for guidance. Envision the life you plan to have and remove your attention away from the things you do not want in your life. Believe that things will get better. Remain calm and have patience. Trust that things will get better.

4. **Am I still loved when I make mistakes?** Yes, you are still loved when you make mistakes. And, you will make mistakes...*learn lessons.* Know that you are always loved no matter what happens in your life. Your Creator may not agree with the choice you have made for yourself...but your Creator understands that you can learn from your mistakes, even if there are consequences - disciplinary actions, punishment. Mistakes teach us to be mindful of our choices the next time. Choose to learn from your mistakes, otherwise, you will keep repeating that same lesson and not move forward with your life. Continuously reinvent yourself and your plans until the day you die. Just see what wonders you can create with your life. You have the courage, strength and determination.

The past cannot be changed; the future is still in your power.

Hugh White

Beautiful Parable.

- Author unknown -

My Wish for you!

Where there is pain…

I wish you mercy and peace.

Where there is self-doubting,

I wish you a renewed confidence in your ability to work through it.

Where there is tiredness or exhaustion,

I wish you understanding, patience and renewed strength.

Where there is fear,

I wish you love and courage.

HURTS

Life-pain is very real and difficult. There are times you may feel as though you have been sliced open and gutted like a fish. Feel your feelings. Know that it is **okay** to feel your feelings. But it is not okay to react negatively and hurt yourself or others. It takes deep soul-work and patience to heal your wounds. Work through your pain *however long it takes.* You are here to heal, forgive and release. Whatever has happened to you in the past has no power in the present, only the power you give it. Do not give the situation one more minute of your life. **Never** define your life by what someone has said or done to you. Remember it is their shame and dishonor, not yours. Redirect your thoughts. **You define you!** Give yourself the love you need each day. Work through your hurts, and find a way to forgiveness in order to release the past and move on. Always Forgive and/or Apologize! Otherwise, you stay stuck in your past misery and miss out on enjoying the present. Whatever it is you are going through, know that you are loved and lovable. Know that your Creator has a plan for you. Keep all these thoughts in mind as you go through life. Believe your life will get better. *Make a healing plan for yourself. Give yourself the love you need each day -You Define You!*

It is not the load that weighs you down, it is the way you carry it.
Susanna York

DIVINE CREATOR...

Grant me the **Serenity** to accept the things I cannot change...

the **Courage** to change the things I can...

and the **Wisdom** to know the difference.

Reinhold Niebuhr

WISDOMS

1. No one person can fix you or save you because it is your soul-work, your lesson. Start now.
2. You cannot seek self-acceptance from anyone; you can only give it to yourself.
3. You cannot see yourself through someone else's eyes; you can only see yourself from within.
4. Mistakes are life-lessons, grow and learn from them. Apologize, forgive, and make amends.
5. Self-love is not to be confused with conceit or selfishness. Conceit and selfishness places oneself above others.
6. If you fall down a 1,000 times, then a 1,000 times you have to pick yourself up.
7. Failure is a signpost to take another path. Learn to spot the red flags earlier next time.
8. Atone for your mistakes, forgive yourself and then move on with a renewed direction.
9. Remember that when one door closes, another will open. And you will see, you were meant to be there. (Sometimes your Creator chooses better for you.)
10. Learn to receive love as well as, give love.

DO

Be Grateful - Count your blessings each day.

Accept Yourself - Believe that it is okay to not fit-in!

Know - that regardless of your life's circumstances, you can succeed!

Maximize the good things, and minimize painful things.

Avoid the Critic "I am not…" as this is creating your belief system.

Be Present – show up for YOU in your life.

Ability is what you are capable of doing.

Motivation is what determines what you do.

Attitude determines how well you do it.

Anonymous

DO LIFE RIGHT!

The challenge is not to be perfect.

The goal is to be whole – to be fulfilled.

Trust your instincts – intuition doesn't lie.

Keep growing until the day you die.

Learn something new each day.

Refuse to do nothing!

Make your life proud.

Keep Imagining.

Keep Exploring.

Be Courageous.

Be Passionate.

Take Chances!

Stay Humble!

Be Creative!

Be Curious!

Be Present.

Go Do!

Be not afraid of life.

Believe that life is worth living,

And your belief will help create the fact.

William James

Honorable Character

- **Be Honorable** – Have good conduct, good actions.
- **Be Proud** – Be Proud of who you are and where you are from.
- **Be Truthful** – Be honest with yourself, family and others.
- **Be Respectful** - Show good character and politeness toward others.
- **Be Responsible** – Be answerable or accountable for your actions.
- **Be Courageous** – Trust you can manage your life. Take a chance!
- **Be Productive** – Use your skills & talents to provide for your income.
- **Be Dutiful** – Carry out your duties to the best of your ability.
- **Be Giving** – Give back your time, energy or money.
- **Be Forgiving** – Forgive others so *you* can move on from the pain.
- **Be Healthy** – Take good care of yourself; body, mind and spirit-soul.
- **Be Calm** – Trust and release. Remain calm and be patient.
- **Be Kind** – You have the power to make others smile ☺

SAINT THERESA'S PRAYER

15th Century

May today there be peace within.

May you trust that you are exactly
where you are meant to be.

May you not forget the infinite possibilities that are
born of faith in yourself and others.

May you use the gifts that you have received,
and pass on the love that has been given to you.

May you be content with yourself
just the way you are.

Let this knowledge settle into your bones, and allow your
soul the freedom to sing, dance, praise and love.

It is there for each and every one of us.

THE PRAYER OF ST. FRANCIS OF ASSISI

12th Century

Lord, make me an instrument of your peace.
Where there is hatred, let me sow love;
where there is injury, pardon;
where there is doubt, faith;
where there is despair, hope;
where there is darkness, light;
where there is sadness, joy;

O Divine Master, grant that I may not so much seek to be
consoled as to console; to be understood as to understand; to be
loved as to love.

For it is in giving that we receive;
it is in pardoning that we are pardoned;
and it is in dying that we are born to eternal life.

Life isn't about finding yourself. Life is about creating yourself.

George Bernard Shaw

What will you create today?

What lies behind us and what lies before us are tiny matters compared to what lies within us.

Henry David Thoreau

Ask and it shall be given to you; seek and ye shall find;

knock and it shall be opened unto you.

Matthew 7:7

Life Plan Journal

(Refer to page 30 for details.)

1. Ask: What are you presently grateful for in your life?

2. Ask: What are your wants, needs and desires? Prioritize them.

3. Ask: Who and what inspires you? Select a role-model etc.

Life Plan Journal

4. **Ask:** What do you enjoy doing? What are your interests or hobbies?

5. **Ask:** What comes naturally to you? List your unique skills and abilities i.e. organizing, problem solving, people person, creative etc. How do you intend to use your skills and abilities to earn a living?

6. **Envision it**: Write a few sentences on what your ideal life looks like? Also, make a vision board with pictures depicting your ideal life.

7. **Want it.** List five goals for your life.

8. **Take Action:** List the steps you need to take? Which one can you do right now? Take that step.

9. **Declare it:** Describe your life's mission and purpose. Only **you** can decide upon your life's mission and purpose. What do you **want** to be doing –versus should be doing. Continuously update your goals throughout your entire life. Begin now.